Psychology of Sales: From Average to Rainmaker

Using the power of psychology to

increase sales

Dennis M. Postema

D1534648

Psychology of Sales: From Average to Rainmaker

Psychology of Sales: From Average to Rainmaker. Copyright ©
2013 MotivationandSuccess.com / Dennis M. Postema. All rights reserved.
No part of this publication may be reproduced, distributed, or transmitted
in any form or by any means unless prior written permission of the author
has been issued. This includes: photocopying, recording, or other
electronic or mechanical methods. An exception may be granted in the
case of brief quotations embodied in critical reviews and certain other
noncommercial uses as permitted by copyright law. For permission
requests, contact the author: PostemaInsurance@netscape.net.

Second edition: March 2014

Contents

Introduction

There are many different types of salespeople in the business world:

- Pushy salespeople who are disliked by most, but still make sales despite causing their customers' skin to crawl

- Quiet, reserved salespeople who that trust their integrity and honesty alone will win them customers, but whose inability to be assertive is sometimes seen as disinterest

- Average salespeople who are occasionally proactive and gently pushy, but more often sit back wanting sales to come to them, which never fails to result in a disappointing year

In the past decade, however, a new breed of sales professional has been making waves throughout the industry: the psychological sales rep. This professional has an entirely new way of dealing with customers. Using basic psychological principles, these reps attract attention, arouse interest, create desire and tap into the buyer's subconscious mind to get to the root of the problem they want solved or need they want fulfilled. The end result is a cleaner, more successful sales process that leaves both the professional and the buyer satisfied.

Approaching sales from a psychological angle wins every time. The sales professional doesn't need to have the most popular product or the most product knowledge; they sell because they understand people and use psychology to communicate effectively with the customer and earn the sale. Even those who aren't in sales can benefit from these lessons to learn how to better sell themselves to hiring managers, negotiate deals and promotions, or even just to sell an old car on Craigslist.

You want to be a rainmaker—one of the most highly successful individuals in sales? Then, you need to shed your old sales method and catch up to what the sales leaders of today are doing.

One: How Does Psychology Work in Sales?

Some people can sell anything. As a sales professional, you might wonder what the secret is to their success. Speaking in only the broadest terms, I'll tell you: they understand the needs of their customers and know how to effectively communicate their products and services as solutions.

On the surface, it sounds simple, but the key to this level of sales success is intensive. It involves developing an understanding of the complex, individualized and layered psychology of your customers while picking up specific psychological cues that can help you master the process of communicating effectively with each client.

One of the best examples of the ultimate salesman, to my mind, is Warren Buffett. You may not think of Warren Buffet as a salesperson, and I think that's the secret to his ultimate success. It's more likely you see him as an advisor, an oracle, an icon—but never as someone who's simply trying to sell you a product.

Yet, look at his annual letters to investors. Within them, not only does he explain the performance of Berkshire Hathaway by discussing some of the decisions made for the holding company, but he also talks positively about the businesses of which the company owns shares, thus helping increase the profits of those underlying establishments. In turn, this drives share prices higher and—you guessed it—increases the value of Berkshire's holdings.

Buffett, like all good salespeople, doesn't raise the red flags often seen in the stereotypical smarmy salesperson. He doesn't sound desperate, or even eager, for sales. He's simply someone you trust who says good things about a company in which he happens to have a financial interest.

In this way, he has mastered the psychology of sales — knowingly or not.

The Ins and Outs of Sales

The process of selling is about more than having a product to hawk and convincing people to buy. In order to become successful in this business, you need to get inside the subconscious minds of your customers and discover why they need the item you sell. Then, get *them* to understand that.

Advertising does this all the time, but not necessarily in the way you might think. Advertisers often focus on creating a lasting impression for their brand and product that rests inside the brains of potential customers. These ads speak about more than just the product; they capture images of the lifestyle your customers want to live, and they tout their product as an integral way to obtain that lifestyle.

No one needs a new car every three to five years, yet many people trade up anyway. Why? Because they long to live the life of sleek sophistication or safe family fun or rugged adventure that each new car offers. Whether the vehicle is practical for their everyday needs, fits into their budget, or will actually help them create the lifestyle they crave doesn't matter; it's how the purchase makes them feel about their life and their future.

Lying underneath this overwhelming desire to create a certain type of lifestyle are the details of the sale. While infinitely less glamorous than the lifestyle design part, these underlying details satisfy another need—the need to do what's "best" or, at least, what the buyer's been told is best. Does it really make financial sense to put $3,500 down on a car, lease it for three years for a slightly smaller payment, and then start all over again when the lease is over? In most cases, the answer is no. Still, each year, millions of people decide to lease their next vehicle rather than buying it. Why? Because they've been convinced it's in their best interest to roll over the lease and get a new model every three years rather than paying less overall by keeping their new car for eight to 10 years and retaining trade-in or resell value.

Sometimes, the basis of need comes from a desire to be safe. Sadly, this doesn't just result in smart purchases but in useless acquisitions that do very little to create or maintain safety and security. I recently spoke with a colleague and friend who bought a new car a few months ago. He's thrilled at all the car's bells and whistles. It's a sturdy car with great ratings and is an appropriate fit with his current lifestyle. In talking about the different approaches to finding the right vehicle, my colleague laughed and told me the story of the manufacturer who called to ask him why he hadn't signed up for an extra service they offered that emails each car owner a printout of their new car's performance every four weeks—for a monthly fee of $19.99. The caller insisted my friend needed the report since it would tell him in advance if anything was going wrong with any of the car's mechanical parts. "You wouldn't want to get stranded on the side of the road, would you?" the salesman asked.

My friend quickly replied that the car in question was only two months old and if the manufacturer of this vehicle was already worried it was going to have problems, maybe he should return it now instead of paying an additional $240 every year for the privilege of being told his car was a dud. Met with silence on the other end of the line, my friend continued by saying, "Call me in five to eight years when this car should be showing some wear and tear, and we'll talk."

After hearing his story, I began asking others who'd bought new cars recently if they were offered the same service and whether they took it. Nine out of every 10 people I spoke with said they had, indeed, purchased similar coverage from their car's maker, thinking it was an important feature to have. Once I pointed out what my friend said, they each looked a little embarrassed for not having thought it through, focusing only on their need to avoid the potential of an unanticipated breakdown.

Ask yourself this question: is this car manufacturer and its salespeople doing anything wrong? No. They're offering a legitimate service that provides a certain kind of protection most people want. They're making sales by using psychology to get into their customers' minds and fulfill a perceived need. It may be unnecessary, but you can't deny that it's ingenious.

Why Use Psychology?

As a sales representative, it's your job to convince shoppers to become buyers. This is a simple three-part process:

1. Show the shopper they have a need.

2. Explain how your product or service fulfills that need.

3. Discover the hidden tipping point inside that turns that particular consumer from a shopper into a buyer.

A sale is ultimately accomplished by using the fundamentals of psychology to create a specific response by tapping into the mental state of the customer. While human nature can be haphazard and unpredictable, psychology is not. It's a science that follows a certain pattern. The same is true for sales.

Every step in the sales process is a mental process— from the attitude of the salesperson, the impression of the customer, the act of arousing attention, awakening curiosity, creating desire, satisfying intangible needs and moving the will. In essence, these are all branches of the psychological process.

Salespeople who rely on logic often find their performance doesn't measure up to their peers who rely on an understanding of psychology. That's because logic and reason are exercises, not impulses. Each is an action in itself, not a spark that ignites a wick and creates a burning desire to act through consumerism. In short, logic and reason aren't compelling enough to make sales. In fact, they aren't compelling at all.

If you want to be as successful a salesperson as your idols, you must learn how to tap into your customers' certain feelings and needs. Remember, a sale is the action and reaction of mind upon mind (yours and the consumer's). If you want to succeed at sales in the modern world, you need to understand your customer in a psychological way, but that's not all. You must also be able to use psychology to project the personal qualities your clients want to see in their sales associates. Only through these two measures will you surpass survival and move onto thriving.

The Psychological Qualities Every Salesperson Must Possess

All salespeople need to start with a foundation of honesty and integrity. Doing so makes the psychological process of exuding confidence and convincing consumers that much easier and effective — because you already truly believe in yourself and your product or service.

There are six core qualities you should focus on when adding or enhancing specific traits that have a psychological advantage to winning sales:

- Confidence: While your mouth is busy saying words, your body is busy talking to your clients. Unless you're in control of your body, it's telling your clients everything you don't want them to know. Do you fear you aren't a good enough salesperson to pull off the big sale? Do you question yourself or your product? Do you let customers intimidate you? The way you stand, speak and even look at a customer tells them all of this and more. If you want to succeed at sales, you need to learn how to use your body language to showcase confidence in yourself, your abilities and, of course, your products.

People rarely follow those who are insecure, self-doubting or continually question themselves even after making a decision. Think about it this way: if you don't believe in yourself and your abilities, why should anyone else? This is especially true in the world of sales. Without confidence in yourself and your product, you are likely to fail.

Of course, this is just one part of the equation. Once you understand it, you enter the next difficult part, which is showing your customers an air of confidence without looking—or acting—cocky. To accomplish this:

o Your body language is vital. Stand straight. Lean forward slightly to indicate interest and engagement. Remember that slouching and swaying may signal weakness.

o Occasionally tilt your head slightly to engage the customer and appear more friendly and interested.

o Don't fidget with paperwork or products as it makes you appear self-conscious.

o Relax your mouth. Tightly pursed lips make you appear disapproving.

However, lips that are too relaxed may signal sadness, apathy or depression.

o Keep your arms open and inviting. Never cross them in front of your body or tense your arms while speaking to a customer. This creates an adversarial mood.

o Have a great handshake. The keys to a good handshake are:

- having a dry palm;

- making palm-to-palm contact;

- keeping your wrist and fingers firm, not like a fish ready to slither out of the other person's grip; and

- taking firm hold of the other individual's hand and pumping up and down no more than three times.

- Maintain a comfortable amount of direct eye contact to showcase confidence to those around you.

A Note about Eye Contact

Believe it or not, there is a right and wrong way to make eye contact with people. The wrong way comes across as intimidating and invasive while the right way is open, confident, trustworthy and inviting.

In general, avoid rigid, unwavering eye contact as it can be intrusive and make people uncomfortable. Instead, look directly into the individual's eyes for four- to five-second intervals. Make sure to time these intervals so you are making direct eye contact when making the most important parts of your sales pitch.

When breaking eye contact, try not to look shifty and allow your gaze to waver from side to side. Look at the individual's other features using slow, controlled eye movements with a normal amount of blinking.

---

o Enthusiasm: When you're truly excited about your job, a meeting with clients or the products you sell, your customers can see it. When they do, they're much more likely to give you a chance to convince them to buy. One warning though: do not try and fake enthusiasm. People will see right through it. Instead, find ways to actually *be* enthusiastic about your products and job. If you can't feel it right now, figure out why. Whether you want them to or not, those feelings come across to your customers.

Enthusiasm is contagious. If you can find a way to exude it, your customers will soak it up and be far more open to listening to you—and buying from you.

• Action and Reaction: In this day and age of product innovation, the wants and needs of your customers seem to be in constant flux. In order to remain on the cusp of their most present concerns, you must stay alert to changes in your customers' attitudes. You can do this by paying attention to remarks they make, including those that might not seem relevant to the situation at hand. Even a mundane comment could give you insight into what they are thinking. In addition, you should:

- Be prepared to handle any situation that arises. Have solutions for multiple problems and practice your outside-the-box thinking skills so they're always sharp.

- Figure out what to say in every circumstance so it'll appear you can think fast on your feet. Not stumbling for the right comeback is essential to making customers feel as if you know what you're talking about and will make them more apt to believe what you say.

- Resourcefulness: One of the best ways for salespeople to show their value to prospects is to present original ideas that solve customers' problems. Being reliable and creative also helps induce impulse buys, which can greatly impact your bottom line. The ability to see problems and show customers how to overcome them is essential to getting those big orders. Train yourself to be innovative when necessary. For instance, I once interviewed a salesperson with a client who wanted to place a large order but didn't have the cash to buy. He had another client with the cash but no space to house the excess inventory. This resourceful salesperson put these two clients together: the one without the cash had an empty warehouse to rent and the other had the money available to pay the fee.

Needless to say, that salesperson managed to get two huge orders from these clients, plus the opportunity to build a relationship all three deemed worthy of a long, prosperous future. Now that's resourcefulness in action!

- Observation: Good salespeople watch the world around them. They can see trends in the marketplace even when they aren't obvious, and they're eager to jump on board before anyone else even notices. But that's not all; a great salesperson also observes customers closely and finds ways to integrate upcoming styles and trends into the client's life in order to generate more sales.

- Initiative: No matter how many motivational morning meetings a company has or incentives they give for top earners, salespeople can't be pushed. They either have a thirst for learning more and doing better, or they don't. Sure, someone can teach you the skills of sales, but only you can decide to take what you've learned and use that knowledge in the real world of sales. Without an inner urge to get to work, even the friendliest and most outgoing salesperson will struggle to survive. Do you have the initiative to take on new challenges and find a way around them? If not, consider why that's lacking within you and make the changes necessary to succeed.

These traits alone won't make your sales quota rise, but they are one part of the two-part system that will. The second part involves understanding the feelings of your buyers and determining how to connect with them.

Appealing to Your Buyers' Emotions

Remember how I said reason and logic aren't sparks that create action? People who take the time to think through a purchase and investigate their options are people who are not currently buying, and may ultimately decide not to buy at all. That's why it's imperative that a good salesperson handle the logic and reason by presenting a strong case for their product while working on the buyer's emotional state to ignite the impulse to purchase. This process is what encourages car salespeople to do everything in their power to keep prospects from walking off the lot without a car. They know that once you leave to "think about it" or "shop around," the odds of you returning are slim. The deal must be made quickly, or it won't be made at all.

The key to success is connecting with the buyer on an emotional level. When you can generate an emotional response from a buyer, you're much more likely to win the sale.

Be Trustworthy

People generally don't enjoy the process of engaging with a sales professional. One reason is because they don't trust them. Ask anyone on the street to tell you a horror story regarding a salesperson and few will hesitate, going straight into a rampage about a bad experience buying a big-ticket item. This can leave sales reps, like you, at a huge disadvantage. That's why you must build a sense of confidence with your buyer that allows them to trust what you're saying and, as a result, what you're selling.

Know Your Product Well

Buyers want to know everything about a product before they buy, especially when it's a big-ticket item. Generally they look to the sales associate for answers to their questions. *Be sure you have those answers.* If you want people to invest in the product you sell, you need to invest time in knowing all of the ins and outs of your product and/or service. You should also spend time practicing answering hard questions before making your sales pitch to a live customer. Until you know everything you can about your product line and have a certain comfort level in fielding questions, you'll find it difficult to make any substantial sales.

Show Consumers How to Use Your Product

People really enjoy infomercials and those home-shopping networks. You may wonder why, and the answer is simple: they allow buyers to see a product being used in a practical way before they decide to buy it. People love seeing firsthand how to use a product. The same is true for your buyer. Give plenty of demonstrations in your presentation. Show customers a variety of ways to use the products you're selling to help them understand just how badly they need the item. Make sure your demonstration stresses how urgent it is that they buy it immediately in order to change their lives in a big or small way. As an added benefit, a "floor show" also displays the quality of your

product and gives customers a sense of its durability. One unique method that can be very successful is developing multiple unexpected ways buyers can use your product. The more you can make the prospect feel as if they need the product, the better shot you have of selling it.

Know What Your Buyer Needs

No matter what you sell, your approach should vary from customer to customer. Rather than concentrating on giving answers, focus on offering solutions to fulfill each client's specific needs. Think about the successful realtor. She understands one buyer may be looking primarily for a house in a great neighborhood. Therefore, even if a house lacks the amenities most people long for, this buyer will overlook that if the location is right. Another, on the other hand, may be most interested in the quality of the neighborhood's schools. Nothing else is as important to this buyer. Still another buyer may consider price the deciding factor.

A real estate agent who does not understand these needs will waste a lot of time schlepping their clients to inappropriate houses, possibly risking a sale altogether.

Unless you know *exactly* what your buyer wants and needs, you will not be able to finish a sale. This requires not only asking many questions, but asking the right questions and figuring out why the customer is interested in your product in the first place. If you do this right, you might even discover the customer's need for your product before they do. Take this data, and use it to communicate persuasive information to them. Then, you'll be able to strike a deal.

Two: What Kind of Sales Rep Are You?

The qualities and attributes of a good salesperson vary. In general, most salespeople exhibit more of an outgoing and charismatic personality. They have an energy and enthusiasm that's infectious, fun to be around, and that makes their prospects feel good. However, there is no one-size-fits-all in sales. Those who are quieter and more sedate can also be successful as their quiet confidence and strength makes their clients feel comfortable and trusting.

None of these characteristics make or break one's ability to succeed in sales. Salespeople can survive with all sorts of personalities. The key is to understand your personality and work with it to connect better with your customers.

What Is Personality?

Personality is the quality of your character. It affects the way you act in a variety of situations. Some adjectives people use to describe personality include:

- honest

- dependable

- moody

- impulsive

- suspicious

- anxious

- excitable

- domineering

- friendly

These are all traits that may be innate to your nature, occurring without thought or effort by you, but they can also be tweaked to enhance your ability to succeed in the sales business. To do so, you must first understand the factors involved in developing personality traits and how they may impact the qualities you're able to develop as well as the way you deal with your clientele.

According to research developed by personality psychologists Robert McCrae and Paul Costa, five major personality traits determine the way people interact with one another and which underlying characteristics individuals exhibit. The Big Five include:

1. extroverted

2. neurotic

3. open to experience

4. agreeable

5. conscientious

1. Extroverted

Extroverts are outgoing, friendly, assertive and upbeat. They seek company and companionship, are talkative and thrive on being around others. Often considered the life of the party, these people are willing to step up and take the lead, telling a joke or story, interacting with everyone they meet and generally being the most gregarious people in a group. This personality trait is especially helpful when excelling at sales since the extrovert is not easily intimidated and can easily connect with all sorts of people in a myriad of situations and environments.

2. Neurotic

Often characterized as impulsive or emotional instability, neuroticism can present itself through anxiousness, hostility, self-consciousness, anger, insecurity and vulnerability. Neurotics can be difficult people to deal with, especially in the sales industry.

They often overreact to emotional stimuli and don't handle stress well. If you lean toward these tendencies, it's important to keep them in check when dealing with customers. While neuroticism can make a life in sales very difficult, it does not have to end your career if you recognize the tendency and work to control it.

3. Open to New Experiences

These individuals are curious, open and enjoy variety. They are open to new experiences and are usually more creative, imaginative, artistic and unconventional. They also tend to be tolerant of other people and their ideas. This is a good characteristic to have in sales since it allows you to change course when needed and get along with a wider range of people.

4. Agreeable

Able to constructively deal with conflict, those who are agreeable are usually considered more trusting, cooperative, modest, compassionate and straightforward. These are all necessary characteristics for a salesperson to possess. Each of them can help you better communicate with clients and make it easier to discover their needs.

5. Conscientious

Conscientious people tend to be diligent, disciplined, organized, punctual and dependable. Customers love these characteristics in a salesperson and, as such, they can help clients trust you completely. Conscientiousness also fosters dependability in the workplace, which tends to play out well in this field.

It's true there is a wide range of possible personality traits, but these five create the core of your—and everyone else's—behavior. Therefore, it's so important for salespeople to adopt the right mix of these character traits as they will determine how you act, react and interact with customers. Of course, that's only the beginning to developing the right type of sales mind.

While these main traits may help establish the basis of your personality, there are other complementary qualities that are important to adopt to succeed at sales.

Additional Traits

Self-Respecting

Insecurity strips you of your ability to sell. While there is no need to be egotistical or conceited to be successful, you must be able to see your own worth and appreciate it. Until you can respect yourself, no one, including your customers, will respect you.

What are some ways to convey self-respect to others? Remember that your physical being and mental state must be working in concert. In other words, your actions must match your thoughts. For instance, if you're always frowning, you will become short-tempered and grumpy. If you force yourself to smile, your entire expression and attitude will change, and that will affect everyone with whom you come into contact.

To elicit feelings of respect from your clients, cultivate one from within. This requires controlling how you act and speak with others and transitioning from a negative mental state to a more positive one. Just as our thoughts can propel us forward toward success, they can also hold us back. All too often we sabotage our own efforts with negative self-talk. Even the smallest comments like, "Boy, that was stupid," or "You should've done better than that," can keep you from doing your best. Practice positive self-talk to combat this tendency. It's the best way to stay on the road toward success and find the courage to move on.

Remember that many of the prospects you see each day have had a negative experience with a sales associate in the past. This has left them skeptical and fearful of being taken advantage of again. A good salesperson must be able to deflect any fear or doubt exuded by potential clients. To do this effectively, they must truly believe they are worthy of the sale and the product or service they're selling is too. In my book, *Unleash Your Mojo*, I explore many different ways you can begin to build your confidence. Three simple exercises include:

- Stop all negative self-talk. When you start your usual loop of negative comments about yourself, stop your mind from finishing the thoughts and focus on the positive opinions you have of yourself.

- Write down some of your most recent accomplishments. Discuss the skills, talents and strengths you used to accomplish them. Look this list over any time you feel your confidence lagging.

- Repeat the following phrase every morning: "I Can. I Will. I Dare. I Do!"

Poised

Poise, or composure, is essential to handling every situation that comes along. When you develop poise, there is little that can get under your skin. You can't be thrown off base by a problem or even a difficult customer. You are self-possessed and thus able to master every situation and find a solution.

While many people associate poise with the physical way a person presents him- or herself, it's much more than that. True poise comes from within. It's the type of mental clarity that allows you to keep your emotions, thoughts and actions in check. Although you may feel rattled internally by something, poise means this internal annoyance won't show on the outside. Poise provides balance to both the mental and physical being.

However, you should not appear so stoic nothing can touch you emotionally. On the contrary, poise does not stop you from feeling or acting according to your natural tendencies. You can be happy, excited, disappointed — any emotion — but your poise helps you exhibit it at reasonable levels, stay in control and allow for fewer mood shifts as circumstances change.

Cheerful

A cheerful attitude is one of a salesperson's most important characteristics. It's practically a magnet for success. No one wants to deal with someone who's grumpy, negative or who speaks only of doom and gloom. While negativity can be a positive trait (as it helps you think of and plan for worst-case scenarios), it should be limited to nothing more than a tool in your box, not a permanent state of mind. Keep negativity under wraps and use it sparingly. Otherwise, you risk alienating people and limiting your sales success.

Show a sunny disposition, and you'll find your customers warming to you. Even those who are gloomy themselves will begin looking forward to your sales calls. Cheerfulness is contagious, and a cheerful customer is more apt to buy.

One warning, though: cheerfulness is not about being a clown or a chronic comedian. Rather, a cheerful person sees the bright side of things. Instead of complaining about a rainy day, they might enjoy the calming sound of the raindrop patter on the roof or the fact that the flowers, grass and trees will explode with color and volume after the storm. Learn to radiate cheerfulness much like the sun radiates light and heat. By doing so, you'll begin exhibiting a whole new side of yourself.

Polite

Courtesy is a valuable asset to the salesperson. I'm not talking about the artificial or dutiful kind, but a true courteous demeanor of someone who values and respects others. This can only materialize when a person feels understanding and sympathy for another and acts kindly to them, giving them the attention and respect they deserve.

When you can see everything from the customer's viewpoint, you'll grow in understanding, and this will show itself in the way you interact with them. Remember, they trust you to help them spend their money; money they worked hard to get and might have had a difficult time saving. When they see you are sincerely polite to them, they'll feel confident you understand them and their needs. That understanding will lead to more sales.

Tactful

Being polite is one thing; being tactful is quite another. As you grow to understand, respect and value your customers more, you'll be in a better position to do and say what is required in order to make a sale. Tact is a strange combination of wisdom and consideration. It is the desire to see another person's point of view coupled with the ability to speak to others as you would want others to speak to you under the same circumstances.

Adaptable

Being able to adjust to changes in your situation and environment is another trait a salesperson should develop. When you're adaptable, it means you're willing and open to helping others, which can only work to increase your sales. Adaptable people can easily switch gears and forge through problems. They're also able to see how others can benefit in a real way from what they have to offer. It's this type of sincere understanding that will help your customers trust you. It isn't always about making a sale, but it is always about helping your customers.

Understanding

Some people just "get" others. They seem to have a core understanding of what people think and feel, and they use that knowledge to win sales. By studying and understanding the basics of human nature, a salesperson can incorporate psychological strategies to increase awareness of their customers and build sales.

Optimistic

Being cheerful isn't the same as being hopeful. A great salesperson should strive to build an optimistic outlook about his or her future. This is done by encouraging yourself to think and believe in the good things to come. Success in life depends on your mental attitude. That means if you expect good to come your way, more often than not, it will. Believe in your success and it will come; doubt it and no matter what you do, success will be fleeting. Doubt in your ultimate success is the same as doubting yourself.

Enthusiastic

Few people really understand enthusiasm. When most of us think of enthusiasm, we picture a cheerleader who is energetic, motivating, hopeful and interested. While enthusiasm is all of these things, it's also an expression of the soul, both in a mental and physical way. It's a deep and devoted passion to something, which means it's not necessarily loud and boisterous.

Think of someone you know who is enthusiastic. They move and act from the very center of their being in a way that impresses others to follow their lead. They show so much excitement for something that others can't help but be interested in learning more. Without real enthusiasm, the sales associate will find it difficult to pull people toward a product and convince them to buy.

Determined

A life in sales is difficult. Without determination, no salesperson can succeed. Determination is created when an ability to tackle tough problems is combined with the courage, boldness, resistance and resilience to go up against those who oppose you. These are the traits that push you forward through the hard times and into the good.

Developing a stubborn tendency is also vital to the salesman. It allows you to develop the tenacity to keep trying even when customer after customer says no. This is the kind of courage that creates a real sales professional—one who can overcome obstacles and make the sale anyway.

Personal Appearance and Presentation

Your voice, personal grooming, clothing and actions are all outward expressions of your inner state. Whether you realize it, the way you stand, walk, look and talk can tell others a lot about you. Sloppy clothing and personal grooming, a jarring or unflattering voice, and a defeated posture will always work against you when it comes to making sales. When your clothes are neat and fit properly, you look presentable and put together. When you speak well, customers will be far more likely to buy from you without some subconscious (or conscious) nagging that something is not quite right with the situation.

Presenting Yourself as a Success

All of these traits, qualities and characteristics are things you're either born with or can develop with some effort. They're worth devoting time toward as they will bring your sales to a level you never dreamed possible.

There are many additional ways of improving your sales through personal presentation. There are certain skills that can also be used in a psychological manner to make clients more receptive to your sales speech. Here are a few things to consider:

- How you carry yourself: As previously discussed, the way you stand and walk can say a lot about how you feel about yourself, your products and even your customer. It's very important for salespeople to develop good habits when it comes to the way they present themselves to customers. First, stand with your heels together and your head held high. Keep your chin slightly drawn in so it does not protrude and your eyes looking forward. Your shoulders should be thrown back, your chest expanded, your abdomen held in. Hold your arms naturally at your sides and, if you use your hands when talking, be sure to steer clear of threatening or domineering motions such as pointing your finger.

- How you shake hands: The Internet hasn't taken over quite yet. Shaking hands is still an important skill and one you should devote some time to learning. Don't begrudgingly surrender a loose, fishlike grip. Appear interested by extending a firm but not rough hand in a way that says, "I like you and you like me."

- How you handle written correspondence: Often, initial sales inquiries will come via email rather than phone or in person. If you handle responses to those emails any less professionally than you would an in-person meeting, you will lose the sale. First, pay attention to how the individual has requested you contact them back. Don't call them if they've asked you to email them. Next, write back as professionally as you'd handle the writing of any official corporate document. Be formal but friendly, using proper English and grammar. Stay away from emoticons such as smiley faces, and remember it's impossible to read tone into an email, so don't try to joke or be sarcastic.

- How you use your voice: One of the most important things you can do with your voice is to speak with expression. Use your voice to convey your excitement and belief in what you sell. Avoid sounding monotone, but make certain you mean what you say and use inflections to prove your point. Never raise your voice. When you get excited, make a point to bring down the tone, since it will likely grow higher with your excitement.

- How you control your eyes: Learn to look people in the eyes when you're speaking to them. However, as previously discussed, do this carefully so you don't make them uncomfortable. Also, remember not to squint or glare because that can make the other person feel as if you're trying to intimidate or overpower them.

- How you dress: Whether we like it or not, we are constantly judged by the way we look. You might not need an expensive suit to make a sale, but you do need to have a clean, neat appearance. You also need to dress to fit the environment. If you're selling tools to a machine shop operator and show up in an expensive three-piece suit, you might not be taken seriously. In this instance, wearing more casual attire will put your customer at ease and make you appear more knowledgeable about the products you're selling. Additionally, while there may not be anything inherently wrong with multiple tattoos and piercings, in some circles and industries these personal modifications are looked down upon. If you're trying to sell your products to a conservative audience, walking into a showroom adorned in tattoos or facial piercings will likely make the customer feel uncomfortable, and an uncomfortable client is not likely to place an order. Do your best to appear in the manner most suited to the current atmosphere.

As you can see, there are many different elements to developing a solid sales mindset. Discovering how to apply psychological techniques to make more sales begins with understanding who you are as a salesperson and developing some of the traits and characteristics mentioned here. However, that's not all. Next, we'll discuss the mind of the buyer to better equip you to discern their needs and give them exactly what they want.

Three: What Are Your Buyers Thinking?

Just as a sales associate has personality traits, character and other qualities, so too does a customer. When you know what these are, you'll be able to tailor your approach accordingly. Not only will this key you in on the individual's needs and priorities, but also how best to convey to them that the product or service you have fulfills all their desires.

Your Client's Personality

Understanding these facets of your client's personality will also allow you to effectively combat objections and answer concerns. When you combine your tailored approach with the details of your own personality that you've developed and tweaked, you become a much more appealing and effective sales professional.

So which of the client's faculties must you begin to understand better? Begin with a person's physical and mental characteristics. Some people tend toward gentle, artistic and emotional, while others are more rugged, strong and unmatched. To fit your client into a general category, consider the following:

- Look at your customer's style of dress, car, accessories and personal grooming.

- Consider their voice, style of speaking, method of listening and reacting to others, and the topics on which they tend to dwell.

Making note of the qualities your customers possess will help you better understand their general character and this can help you better tailor your sales approach.

However, it's never good to make assumptions based on such broad definitions of character, which is why you must also look at individual traits to complete your client profile. Think of yourself as an investigator. You want to get the big picture first, but before making any assumptions, you need to learn more and explore the evidence.

One of the greatest advantages a salesperson can have is a true understanding of the customer. Once you can get a handle on the customer's position and character, you'll be in a much better position to tweak your sales approach to meet that specific personality or character.

The Social Buyer

Social beings are often ruled by their attraction to others. This can be a friendly attraction or a sexual one. Understanding the type of social interaction a customer feels most comfortable with can have a big impact on how you deal with that sale.

For instance, a customer driven by their desire for sex will not give you the time of day if a member of the opposite sex shows up during your presentation, because your product is not answering their ultimate need. However, if you bring along a good-looking colleague to the appointment, he or she may be able to hold the customer's attention long enough for you to tap into their other needs and desires.

On the other hand, those with a marital inclination (the desire to please their spouse) will be more interested in your product if their spouse likes it. Ignore the spouse or their wishes and you will lose the sale. Too many car sales associates forget the importance of the spouse when trying to interest a buyer. If the salesperson doesn't include the spouse in the conversation or fails to excite the spouse, the sale can be ruined if they're dealing with someone with a high marital inclination.

Still others may value friendship above all else. Fail to develop some sort of friendship with the customer — even a casual business friendship — you won't be able to break through and make the kind of sales you deserve with this specific customer.

There are many different ways social beings interact. Failing to determine which inclinations drive them will result in shortchanging yourself when dealing with that particular customer.

The Self-Interested Customer

The self-interested customer gauges everything you say and offer based on how it will affect them on a personal level. Promise increased life, health, riches and more to this group of people and you'll gain a customer. These types of people are excellent customers for health-related products and services. They fear illness, are often obsessed with health and will do just about anything to get the most out of life.

The self-interested customer also likes to win, so be careful not to argue with them, even when they're wrong. A person exhibiting these qualities is so adamant and focused on not losing the argument they may forget the bigger picture altogether. Always avoid a dispute with this personality type. Hook them with kindness, gentleness and lots of promises, that you can fulfill, for a better life.

The Bargain Hunter

This type of customer is always looking for the best deal. Unless a bargain can be had, they aren't interested. They may seem miserly, but if presented with a great deal, they'll grab it. In a sense, the discount or compromise in terms is what they're most interested in buying—more so than the product. In selling to such a customer, be sure to "prove" how your product is going to ultimately help the customer make or save money. Without solid proof, this customer will pass by your product, no matter how good it is.

The Shrewd Shopper

A simple sale price or bargain deal isn't enough for the shrewd shopper. This cunning client is always out to double-deal everyone. Be wary when dealing with this type of customer. They're always looking for a way to outsmart you and can succeed if you aren't careful. Don't fall for their tricks simply to make a sale. Take control of the sales call and know your limits before walking into a meeting with a cunning client. Otherwise, you may strike a deal that looks good on paper only to discover you've lost on the entire deal, while the customer made big gains at your expense.

The Cautious Consumer

The cautious consumer needs to be dealt with very gently and honestly. This person may be so afraid to make a move they actually miss out on good opportunities. Your job as a sales professional is to carefully pick and choose the deals you bring to this customer and develop a level of trust with them. The cautious consumer is not likely to act fast on any large-scale purchase, so trying to speed things up with the limited time or quantity approach is not going to work and can actually make the client suspicious. Instead, advise this customer in advance of upcoming deals so they can think it over and run the numbers themselves. Being patient with a cautious customer may be difficult for some salespeople but can be very beneficial in the long run. This customer can't be rushed—trying to do so will only result in failure for the sales representative.

The Show-Off

You know the type: the customer who loves to show off his newest acquisition. He loves flattery and praise, but is very sensitive to criticism. By allowing the customer to be "full of himself," the salesperson may appear to be giving the customer the upper hand, but in actuality, that's the best way to take control of the sales call. Show-offs are so sure you can't make a living without their purchases, they're more willing to buy than other personality types.

The Confident Client

These customers don't rely on anyone for success. They're capable of attaining it alone, and they know it. Confident clients want their own way and don't stop until they get it. So, how do you deal with this type of customer? Don't ever try and force the sale. Acknowledge the customer's ability to recognize the right product or service on their own, and complete the presentation in a more impersonal way—just a matter-of-fact presentation of options with no opinions or strong sales tactics from you. This leaves the entire matter in the customer's hands. They like to believe they've come up with the decision to make the purchase without any prodding or cajoling from the salesperson, so resist the urge to actually "sell" your product line. Offer the facts, sit back, and let the customers figure out how it will benefit them.

This can be difficult for most salespeople since they're so used to using flattery and their expertise to convince the customer to buy. That approach simply will not work in this case. The confident client takes the lead and the sales representative who can allow him or her to do that will benefit greatly.

The Faculties of Application

We've been talking a lot about how customers think and how you can use their emotional and psychological tendencies to your benefit during a sales call. But that's not the end of the story. You must also consider how a customer's personality traits impact their decision to accept or deny your sales approach. The short answer is that it depends on two factors:

1. The firmness of the customer's decision making

2. The continuity or patience a customer uses when making a decision

Firmness

Some people just cannot be moved. They know what they want, they know what they don't want, and they can't be persuaded otherwise. Stuck in their ways, these individuals are devoted to their decision, even when it's wrong. Trying to change their mind is like banging your head against a wall. Actually, that's not true—because if you bang your head against the wall hard enough, you'll actually make a dent in the wall—but you'll never budge these intractable souls.

The only way to change the minds of those firm customers is to let them "win" on their terms while presenting your thoughts and opinions in an entirely different manner. Instead of trying to change this customer's mind, simply get their mind off the question at hand and plan an attack from another angle that will go unnoticed. It's impossible to batter down the stone wall they've built. You must either find a way over, under, or around it.

For example, let's say you're in the business of selling cell phones. Your prospect loves her phone from Maker A and is convinced it's the perfect phone for her. Rather than telling her why she's wrong, you're better off acknowledging her position, and then transitioning from telling her why the phone is right for her to why it's right for others. In doing so, be sure to mention all the benefits of the phone that Maker A doesn't provide but that you know this customer would want. Once you stop selling and trying to convince her she is essentially wrong and start focusing on the product and its benefits, the client is more likely to talk herself into needing what you have for sale.

Continuity

People who like continuity generally don't like change. They're most comfortable doing things the same way they've always done them. Even when technology or other innovations create products that will make their lives easier, they resist.

Before you figure out how to tackle this individual's roadblocks, it's important to understand why they are that way. For some, it could be fear of the unknown or skepticism about newly manufactured goods. For others, it may be that they wish to retain a sense of control, and new products or routines introduced into their lives take away that control—at least temporarily. Still others might be this way out of sheer laziness. You must try to figure out the reason behind your customer's desire to cling to what they have if you want to effectively sell them what they need.

One way to get through the customer's fear, need for control or laziness is to show both products side by side and illustrate how similar they are. Give them a demonstration of the simple changes while punching your talk with the major changes and positive influence the new product will have on their quality of life. Remember, the goal is to downplay the amount of change in process they're in for, not the impact of the product.

Another useful approach is to use words like *conservative* and *established* when introducing new items to a continuity-loving customer who's skeptical of change and new manufacturing—you know, the ones who think nothing is made as well as it was back in "their" day. This customer loves the tried and true and will resist any type of change, so avoid trying to offer new things on a regular basis. Stay with what sells already and slowly introduce newer products.

Challenging Character Traits

A person's character will determine what they buy and how they buy it. It can also lead a good salesperson in their approach with that customer, giving clues as to how best to get the sale.

While most of your clients will be nice, normal and easy to help—there are some who have special character traits that need a delicate approach. These traits include:

Argumentative

Some people just want a good fight. Argumentative people find it fun to argue with sales associates, dispute all claims and try to best them in general knowledge about the industry. Often, and quite sadly, they want to argue for the sake of arguing and not for the sake of truth or advantage. If you take these types of buyers too seriously, you'll find yourself frustrated. Let them enjoy the argument and give them victory over a few minute points. Have grace and good humor during the entire discussion so it doesn't devolve. Once they've seen you yield to a few points, they'll be more willing to be gently coaxed along the main lines of your selling talk. Have fun with this buyer. Don't take them too seriously, but don't dismiss them out of hand, either. Above all else, give them the time and space to voice their argument. This will make the sale much easier.

Conceited

As you gain more confidence in your sales ability, you'll find it much easier to deal with conceited individuals. This particular type of buyer is very full of him- or herself and can intimidate a newer salesperson. While this buyer may think they know it all and, subsequently, that you know very little, they can be relatively easy to influence simply by deferring to their "expertise" and making them feel as if they're doing all the selling. When buyers such as this feel as though you're deferring to them, they'll be much more likely to listen to your sales talk, even though they might pretend they aren't.

Stubborn

The stubborn buyer often resembles a stone wall that you can't push through. No matter how hard you try, this individual seems impervious to your efforts. Luckily for you, this isn't actually the case. While the stubborn buyer may seem impenetrable, they can usually be convinced to buy if you try some unexpected, unusual tactics. Generally speaking, this individual will get hung up on one point and that will be the sole focus of their stubbornness. Instead of trying to overpower this customer's will on that point, focus on other aspects of the deal or product that could prove to be tipping points.

Irritable

Irritable people must be handled in a gentle and even-toned manner. Never allow this type of buyer to fluster or anger you. Above all else, never raise your voice with this type of buyer, even if they raise their voice at you. Call on your poise to help you remain cool and confident. Speak evenly and remain positive, but don't become excessively cheerful or enthusiastic in an attempt to combat their irritability as it will likely make it worse. Your goal is not to soothe the irritable buyer, an action that often exacerbates their irritation. It's to remain emotionally detached from their irritation so they feel comfortable letting down their defenses with you and are more willing to listen to your sales pitch.

Roughshod

This buyer wants to be in control and isn't afraid to run right over you in the process. Stay firm and keep your emotions in check. Do not allow yourself to be rattled by this buyer's forceful and dismissive demeanor. Remain firm and calm and always keep in mind what your bottom line is for making the sale.

Every buyer brings to the sale his or her own character traits. These traits are the deciding factor determining whether the client will be drawn into your pitch. By understanding how a buyer thinks, feels and acts you can cater the delivery of your presentation and approach to get the reaction you want: a sale.

Now that you understand what makes individual buyers act and react so differently to your pitch, let's take a look at what makes buyers actually buy certain products and services.

Four: Why Do People Buy?

America has a consumer-driven culture. Last year alone, Forbes estimated the average American spent more than $43,000 on—are you ready for this?—"stuff." Now, some of that "stuff" was needed, but a lot of it consisted of excess items and impulse purchases the consumer simply wanted.

As a salesperson, you want to tap into the minds of buyers in order to figure out why they buy one product over another. Doing so will help you figure out how to get them to purchase your product or service over your competitor's.

I've found there are two major customer mindsets that affect the type of purchases made by a consumer: the voluntary mindset and the involuntary mindset. Both are equally important in helping a consumer make a buying decision. The difference is the driving force behind each.

The Involuntary Mindset of a Buying Consumer

The involuntary, or subconscious, mind is where feeling and desire are housed. While most people like to believe they make buying decisions with their intellect, that's simply not true. For most of us, the decision to purchase a new car, home or even an outfit is made more because of how the buy makes us feel rather than whether the item makes intellectual sense. The involuntary buyers do much of the work in talking themselves into items, too. They want a certain feeling, lifestyle, appearance, sense of belonging or quality of life, and when they see something they think can help deliver on that primary need, they rationalize the purchase so it seems as though it's a logical choice— even if it isn't.

When dealing with a customer who is primarily led by his or her involuntary mind, remember they often act on impulse and follow their urges and desires more readily. They're often easygoing and as long as you understand their primary, overarching desire, you can determine how your product might help fulfill this.

The Voluntary Mind of the Buyer

The voluntary mind, on the other hand, doesn't cater to a buyer's feelings, but rather, to the facts of the purchase. If Spock were a consumer, he'd be of a voluntary mind. For consumers who are primarily led by their voluntary mind, an emotional attachment to a certain lifestyle or image has little bearing on whether they buy. For those with more control over their involuntary mind, wants and desires are pushed aside for a more practical decision.

This consumer can't be convinced to buy just because everyone else wants a particular item. In fact, it would be impossible for them to care any less about how the purchase will make them look to others. They respond best to solid reasoning regarding the purchase.

Knowing which type of mind has control over an individual consumer can be very important to the salesperson. After all, if your buyer is controlled by the involuntary mind, then you want to gear your sales talk toward the emotional aspect of the sale, such as how the item will make them feel about themselves or how others will react to it. Focusing on the practicality the voluntary mind seeks will result in failure—and vice versa. While the involuntary-minded customer will not be swayed by the amount of money saved over the next five to 10 years on maintenance and fuel costs by purchasing a more efficient vehicle, the voluntary-minded person will be persuaded heavily by such knowledge.

Why People Buy

In the last section, we touched on the major mindsets that affect your prospect's buying behavior, but let's look at some of the underlying aspects of these mindsets in more detail.

If you want to make a sale, it's vital you understand the psychological drivers hidden inside your prospects. It's also helpful to know the reasons why people buy at all. For years, psychologists have been studying the mental reasoning people use to justify a purchase—so have marketing and advertising gurus. Armed with this knowledge, they've been able to gear some of the most effective advertising campaigns ever dreamed of toward certain types of consumers.

Now, you can take the same knowledge and use it to increase your own sales potential. Here are 10 of the top reasons why people buy and suggestions on using these factors in your next sales appointment.

1. Most people think with their emotions, not their
    brains: The vast majority of sales are made
    because of a feeling, a perceived need or an
    emotion, not as a result of rational thinking. If
    you can pinpoint the customer's emotional hot
    button, you're much more likely to make the
    sale. Consider the increase in baby-proofing
    products over the last 20 years. When most of us
    were toddlers, our parents may have had a
    single baby gate at the top of the stairs and little
    else to keep our curiosity in check. That's no
    longer the case. Today's parents have specially
    designed locks, latches and gates to keep their
    young children out of every room, drawer,
    cabinet, outlet and staircase around the house.
    This billion-dollar business isn't just about
    products anymore, either. Now there are service
    providers who come into a home, give it a
    complete baby inspection, and then childproof

every corner of the house. Why? Are our houses more dangerous than our parents' homes were? Of course not. If anything, with product recalls and more stringent safety measures, they're safer than ever before. The increase in baby-proofing sales is because parents need—as they always have—to feel safe about the environment their baby is in. Over the years, as a result of this need, more and more product innovation has occurred, making it easier to fulfill this desire. This brings us a good example of emotional buying. It isn't *fact* that's getting people to buy these products; it's their fear. Use that same strategy to convince your customers of the importance of what you sell.

2. People are egocentric: Many purchases are made once this question has been answered: What will it do for me? Consumers are often consumed by ego when it comes to making purchases. They

want assets that will make them look better to the world, feel better about themselves and give them pleasure. Figure out how the products and services you sell can make your customer feel or look better, and you are often guaranteed a sale.

3. People look for value: Value and price are not the same. You may have the lowest price in town, but if people don't see value in what you offer, you won't make a single sale. Yet someone selling something completely unnecessary may be able to get three times the price for their item simply because people see some degree of value in it. Create more value in the mind of the consumer with regard to your price, and you will see your sales increase.

4. People think in terms of people: Consumers want to feel as if they're connected to other people. Whether it's a celebrity they want to emulate or a neighbor they want to keep up

with, people want the feeling this purchase will somehow connect them to others. That's why testimonials and personal stories or photos work so well for salespeople. Think about diet ads. It's not the scientific information that grabs the buyers' attention—that simply serves to help them justify a decision they made impulsively. Instead, it's the before-and-after photos that seal the deal. Someone who is overweight may listen to a doctor drone on about how fat cells and metabolism work, but what they're most interested in is changing from a size XL to a size S. From wearing elastic-waist pants to skinny jeans. When they see before-and-after photos, they feel a connection to that average person who appears to be just like them. That motivates them to buy.

5. People love to spend money: Shopping isn't a chore, it's an activity. It's a common pastime for

people of all ages and income groups. One hundred years ago the average person generally bought something because they needed it, not because they wanted it. Today's consumer couldn't care less if they need the product you're selling. Generally, as long as you can make them feel like they want it, they will buy it.

6. People yearn for more: Today, dissatisfaction reigns supreme. The more we have, the more we tend to want. Look for ways to fulfill a customer's wants and desires, and they will come back to you for more.

7. People use their senses when buying: People are generally sensory beings. While online sales have increased in recent years, there are many who still want to see and touch brand new products before deciding to buy. Yes, they may order that new dining set online, but not before they've visited a few showrooms to get a feel for

the quality, comfort and usability. Remember to use sensory details when trying to make a sale. Allow the buyer to touch the item, smell it and even try it out. Basically, let them experience it in a sensory way. Think about the last time you bought a new car; didn't you just love the way it felt to sit in the seats? And how about that new-car smell? Nothing beats that. These are all sensory triggers that made you buy that car rather than the used one down the street that was half the price.

8. People tend to follow the crowd: I once lived in a neighborhood where it seemed like once one person on the block bought something, everyone else followed suit. I bet your neighborhood operates about the same way. If Neighbor A puts up a fence, I could rely on at least five to eight more fences going up within the month. Or maybe Neighbor B puts in a new pool. You can

bet three to five more pools are going to be added to backyards that summer. It isn't just teenagers who follow the crowd; most adults do it too. This is a great trend for sales professionals—if you know how to leverage it.

Let me give you the perfect example. Two months before I moved, one of my neighbors hired a wonderful landscaper to come in and plant trees, design a beautiful flower garden and install a decorative pond to create a backyard paradise. Within three days of its completion, enough time for all the neighbors to have been invited over to see the masterpiece, the landscaper started knocking on doors to let everyone know what the neighbor had done and offered a great sales pitch for his design services. Needless to say, he was busy for months from the work he generated simply by playing one neighbor's yard against another's. Each job got more detailed and expensive until our entire neighborhood resembled a mini-arboretum. It was amazing to watch my neighbors try to outdo one another. What shocked me the most was the fact that no one had even thought of adding so many decorative touches to their property until one neighbor did it, and the landscaper walked around telling everyone about it. And while everyone else in the neighborhood thinks of him as a landscaper, I think of him as a master salesman. He knew that people had a tendency to follow the crowd and used those psychological traits to drum up business—lots and lots of business!

9. People need to justify their decisions to buy: Consumers may make purchases because of feelings, but then they need to justify those purchases with facts so they don't feel buyer's remorse. When making your sales pitch, be sure

to include plenty of facts to help make their decision easier to swallow when rationality starts creeping back in.

10. People are suspicious: It may seem like people will buy anything these days, but that's not completely true. Most consumers remain skeptical of salespeople and deals that "are too good to be true." Be sure to back up your claims with statistics, survey results and even testimonials. Above all else, do not appear to be smarmy or you will fail.

These are just some of the psychological reasons why people buy things. While there are certainly plenty of others, these are the main traits to keep in mind when trying to determine how to attempt a sale with a particular group or individual.

Five: The Five Commandments of a Presale Strategy

Understanding your own sales style and then learning more about what your buyer is thinking, and how that relates to the sale, are all important factors to help you develop a winning sales approach. However, those are secondary to the first step you should take, which is to devise a presale strategy. This is quite a process that involves mapping out a complete campaign or setting the groundwork on which to build.

Commandment #1: Know Thy Product

Even if you do only one thing as a presales strategy, it should be to know your product. If you don't know your product or service inside and out—better than you know the back of your hand—then you will absolutely never be a success. I know it sounds harsh, but sometimes tough love is exactly what's necessary. If you do not know your product, not only will that undermine your confidence but it will also prevent you from satisfying your client's quest for knowledge. Finally, it will give you less creativity in developing ways to show your client how your product can solve their problems or satisfy their desires. I can't stress this enough: if you don't know your product, you will fail.

One warning here: just because you have all of this information does not necessarily mean you have to share it. A sales professional who drones on and on about every facet of the product will only bore the customer. The important thing here is that you can answer any questions that arise in a logical, knowledgeable way.

Commandment #2: Know Thy Industry

Even if you do know everything about your product, from how the wood is harvested, how many nails it contains, or what the designers were eating for breakfast when it was developed, if you don't know the surrounding industry, you could still face failure.

When you know the industry, you also know your competitors and their products. This will allow you to show your customers why your product is better, which is a fundamental aspect of getting more sales.

The other important part of knowing your industry is to gain the ability to identify changes and trends. Doing so will allow you to adapt your sales pitch so you can convey why your product is still relevant, even in a changing industry.

Commandment #3: Know Thy Target Customer

We've covered a lot of ground regarding getting to know your customers and figuring out their personal character traits and buying preferences, but these are all steps you take after you meet your customer face to face. Before you can do that, you have to get your message out to people who could conceivably be purchasers of your product or service. To do this, think about the types of people for whom your product or service is relevant. Consider their trade, how or where they conduct their business, what they like and don't like, and so on. There's nothing you can learn about your customer's professional and personal life that is valueless. Every nugget of information you glean is just one more thing to help you find your clients and streamline your sales approach.

Marketing experts spend billions of dollars each year for the purpose of collecting information on buying trends and spending data for this exact reason. Have you noticed that lately it's becoming more difficult to find a store that doesn't push their preferred customer card on you? They promote the card because it allows customers access to special sales and discounts, but the real reason merchants want consumers to use them is so they can gather information about the consumers' buying habits. This information helps merchants design advertisements, sales and other marketing tools to convince customers to buy more.

Commandment #4: Know Thyself

Once you learn everything you can about your product and your target customer, it's time to get to know yourself. Again, we discussed your selling styles and personality in the first chapter, but now it's time to figure out what may be holding you back in your sales approach.

Fear is the biggest enemy for most sales representatives. They fear being told no. They fear being unable to answer the clients' questions. They fear failing. Stop allowing fear to stand in your way. Adopt an attitude that says, "I know I'm honest, and I know that my product is good. If this person doesn't want what I have to sell, I'll find someone who does."

Fear can be an insidious thing, holding you back from achieving any sort of success. When you give in to your fears, you actually weaken your personal power and allow others to control you.

Those who succumb to the fear of failure never give themselves a chance to succeed. They convince themselves to believe in a set of reasons why they cannot succeed. They tell themselves things like:

- I'm not good enough for that job.

- I'm not successful enough for that group.

- I'm not smart enough for that career.

Stop allowing your fears to get the better of you. Customers can smell your fear a mile away. Get over these fears as part of your presales strategy development so you can walk into every sales call fearless. Know you have a great product to sell and if the customer turns you down, then someone else will see the benefit of buying it.

Believing in yourself and your product is the key to success. It really is just a state of mind, and once you can break through that chasm of fear and believe your clients need what you're offering, they will begin believing that too. Remember, you must convert yourself before you can convert your customer.

Commandment #5: Know Thy Approach

The second phase of the presale process is to secure an appointment with a potential customer. In many cases, the customer will come to you. Let's say you're a real estate agent. If you handled Commandment #3 correctly, you can expect to get a call from a potential buyer asking for information on a specific house. At this point, many agents will give out only minimal information. They think doing so will convince the caller to come into the office so they can chat about their needs to help them find the absolute best house.

The stage between the presale approach and actual customer approach is a very delicate time in your sales relationship. There is a fine line between giving the caller the answers they seek and getting them to agree to meet with you. Failing to answer their questions may seem like a good idea, as the withheld information could act as an incentive to get them to come in. Conversely, it may frustrate the caller and leave them looking elsewhere for satisfaction. Giving too much information, however, may lead them away before you ever have the chance to find out what they're really in the market for.

Other salespeople have similar problems. Car sales professionals are often told by customers they're just shopping around and do not want to get into any serious sales discussions, while other types of salespeople may be put in a holding pattern by customers seeking to gain the upper hand. These are all scenarios that can erode a sales rep's confidence and leave them feeling as if the client is in charge.

Allowing a client to take the lead in the sales meeting can be detrimental to the salesperson's ability to land the sale. It puts the sales professional in a passive mode that's often difficult to break out of. Your mental attitude and physical expression instinctively influence the conduct of other people, including your customer. That's why it's so important to take the lead during sales discussions.

Tips for Setting Up the Sale

Not sure how to set up a sale? Here are a few tips to get you started:

- Keep in touch with previous customers: Just because a customer hasn't bought anything in a while doesn't mean they never will. Even former prospects, those who you thought you would make a sale with but didn't, could still be future customers. Maybe they walked into your furniture store looking for a new bedroom suite but ended up buying somewhere else for less after you managed to convince them of how necessary the suite was. Stay in touch without being harassing or overbearing by sending periodic sales notices, a birthday card, anything to keep in touch. Staying in touch builds relationship and relationship is what brings customers back through your doors.

- Keep track of prospects and sales: There's probably nothing more deadly in the sales game than working on a deal only to let it slide through the cracks due to your inability to keep track of what you're doing and who you're dealing with. Stay on top of every lead and follow-through on every sales call—no matter how insignificant it may seem.

- Use innovation to your benefit: Use email, text, social media and your website to grab a customer's attention. Be careful not to become obtrusive or a bother, but do send out periodic messages, alerts or data your customers may find important or interesting.

Using these basic strategies to lay the foundation for presale groundwork can dramatically increase your bottom line by developing a good working relationship with your customers.

Six: The 10 Steps of the Purchase

Now that you know why people buy what they do, it's time to talk about the inner process they go through before making purchases. Large or small, every purchase is generated by a 10-step buying process that happens inside the buyer's head. It can take seconds for the entire 10-step process to take place, or it can take months. The timetable depends on the type of purchase as well as the personality of the consumer.

For example, you may decide in less than a minute to grab that spontaneous purchase at the end of the aisle at the grocery store, but it may take you weeks or months to decide whether to buy a new car and which one to get. Regardless, your mind will still follow these 10 steps in order to talk yourself into either purchase.

Step 1: Involuntary Attention

You know when you're paying attention to something because it grabs your thoughts and feelings. Did you ever realize you could involuntarily give something your attention? It's true. Involuntary attention is a reflex or nervous response to stimuli. It's also the very first mental step in the process of making a purchase.

A sudden sound, taste, smell or other sensation may grab your attention without you even realizing it. Maybe you notice an advertisement in the paper as you scan the pages. Your conscious mind may not register the ad, but your subconscious does, which creates a set of involuntary internal reactions during which your brain begins contemplating the purchase even before you realize you noticed the ad in the first place. Oddly enough, you may consciously notice the ad after you've made the decision to buy and just chalk that up to a coincidence.

Step 2: The First Impression

Once the involuntary attention response is activated, a buyer will suddenly notice the product, service or salesperson. Their attention is now on the thing being considered. It's this very first impression that sets the stage for the rest of the deal. When a customer first notices you or your product, the initial response they get will become imprinted in their memory, and they'll judge all other conversation and demonstration on that impression. That's why it's so important to consistently practice good posture, eye contact and positivity—because your body might giving them a response while you aren't even aware of it.

People are influenced by this first impression much more than they'll admit. Even if the product being pitched is perfect in every way, if the client's first impression of it or the salesperson is poor, a sale will never come to be. A favorable first impression will smooth the way for a successful awakening of the later mental stages. An unfavorable impression, while it may be removed and remedied later, will nevertheless handicap the sales professional's approach.

Step 3: Curiosity

Humans have an instinctual need to explore the unknown. We're attracted to the mysterious, different, puzzling and fascinating. If you, as a sales professional, can introduce some fact or tidbit that arouses the buyer's curiosity, you'll be able to gain their attention and interest, which can ultimately lead to a sale.

Step 4: Interest

Deeper than curiosity, interest actually elicits practical awareness of how a product or service can be used to better one's life. Curiosity is instinctual, but interest is acquired. It develops over time as you use your personal ideas and experiences to evaluate the world around you. What interests us will depend a great deal on our personal tastes, experience, temperament, prejudices and so on. This is important for the sales professional to understand and use. What interests one customer will not interest another, at least, not in the same way. To grab a customer's interest, you'll have to make your presentation in a way he or she can connect with. If a customer's interest is in saving money, then explaining how the purchase will save money in the long run will be a winning strategy.

Step 5: Consideration

This mental state is defined as "an examination, inquiry or investigation into anything." It's the stage in the purchase process that follows curiosity and interest and lends itself to inquiring more about the product or service being offered. This is the "I think I'll look into this matter" stage of the buying process. You know your customers have reached this stage when they begin asking more questions. They want to learn as much as they can and see if it's worth their time and money. This is when the real selling work begins. The customer has passed through the passive interest state into an active interest state and is seriously considering the purchase. This is the time to stress your best selling points. If you're successful at this part, the buyer will move onto the next stage of the process: imagining him- or herself owning what you're selling.

Step 6: Imagination

The ability of customers to see themselves driving that new car off the lot or living in that new house is an important part of the buying process. Without the ability to create vivid pictures in their mind, the buyer will not be led to make the purchase. Buyers must be able to imagine the positive aspects of the purchase in order to actually make the sale. The successful salesperson understands how important this stage is and will fuel the fire of imagination with plenty of suggestions. Imagination is the channel through which suggestion reaches the mind. Salespeople who, by using clever wordplay, arouse the imagination in prospective customers are much more successful than those who don't.

Step 7: Desire

Desire is the drive that says, "Buy it," even when a customer knows they shouldn't. For some people the desire to buy is stronger than their common sense and thus, completely overrides it. For others, desire is just one aspect in their decision-making process. Either way, until the customer feels some desire for the item or service up for sale, they will not buy. So, it's vital for the sales professional to find a way to create some degree of desire in their product.

Step 8: Deliberation

Once interest has given way to desire, the customer begins deliberating the pros and cons of making the purchase. This is the stage where the customer balances facts with feelings to determine the validity of the purchase. For some more impulsive buyers, this will be a very short stage. For those less likely to give in to their emotions, it could take much longer. Knowing your customer can help you foresee how much information and what type of information to offer to help make these internal deliberations go more smoothly.

It has been said, "People seek not reasons, but excuses for following their feelings." Our minds are controlled by motives and the strongest motive wins, so be sure to help motivate your customer toward the purchase using some of the strategies offered here.

Step 9: Decision

After deliberation comes the decision. During this short phase, a customer either decides to buy the product or not. This isn't always an easy part of the buying process and can leave some prospects stuck for a while. Until a final decision is made, the final step in the buying process cannot, and will not, happen.

Step 10: Action

Once a solid decision to buy has been made, the only thing left to do is write up the contract and finish the sale. This is the final action step of the buying process.

Who knew that every time a person makes a purchase, they go through these 10 psychological steps? It may take mere seconds for the customer to move through each of these stages, but no matter how big or small the purchase, each of these mental steps are followed.

When you find a customer struggling to make a decision regarding a purchase, take a closer look at where they are in the buying process. Once you recognize which step they're stuck on, you can offer the help necessary to move them along the buying path.

Now let's take a look at a more practical part of the selling process: the approach. How you approach a customer has a big impact on whether a sale is made or lost. Let's take a closer look at this all-important psychological step to selling anything.

Seven: Approaching Customers without Scaring Them Away

If you're planning to use the psychological techniques described in this book, you've already figured out you will have to glean certain information from your customers to communicate in a winning manner. This all begins when you first approach the client.

Making that initial contact is not only the most important part of the sales call, but it can also be the hardest. There's an old saying in the sales world that goes something like this: "The first five minutes of speaking with a customer will either make or break the sale." That may be a cliché, but the truth remains—first impressions do count. Without a positive first impression, you won't be able to pull off this, or any, sale.

It doesn't matter whether you're making a sales call or you're welcoming a customer into your store. The key to making a good first impression is acknowledging the customer, looking for clues, listening to their needs, asking the right questions and then listening some more.

Acknowledging the Customer

Every first approach toward a customer should be relaxed, easy and friendly. Never walk up behind a customer. Make certain to always come in from a sideways or front-facing entry point.

Also, don't come in with sales guns ablaze. Simply begin by saying "good morning" or "good afternoon." Then stop. This leaves the customer a moment to relax and respond. Nobody likes a pushy salesperson who begins with the polite equivalent of "How can I help you spend your money today?" Even the seemingly innocent "What can I do for you today?" is seen as overly pushy by many customers who may want to shop quietly without feeling the need to explain themselves. Remember, no matter your intention, both of these approaches can make a customer tense and make them think you require a commitment of a purchase in order to even ask a few questions.

There is a fine line between acknowledging a customer and pressuring them. Be friendly and calm with your initial contact. Never pounce. Give the customer a chance to walk into your store, look around for a moment, and then approach them in a friendly manner.

I do have one warning; some customers come in with questions and while you never want to ignore them and risk losing the sale, you also don't want to seem overly eager or aggressive. Instead of making a beeline to them as soon as they enter, grab an item or two from the back that you can take to the racks to "put away."

That way, you can approach the customer without them thinking you see them as "marks" and are coming in for the hard sell. By appearing that you're doing something else but have interrupted your process just to touch base with them, you appear much less aggressive and ready to pounce, and much more helpful.

Looking for Clues

Every customer gives certain signs when it comes to what they're looking for. Take the time to try and read your customer. Maybe you overhear a conversation between two partners that goes something like this:

Partner A: "But we need a new washer and dryer. The bigger one will hold more clothes and the big comforters."

Partner B: "I know, but we only have $1,000 to spend. I don't think we can get what we really want for that amount of money."

You now have some important clues to help you tailor your sales pitch to both partners:

1. They use a large-sized comforter, which may retain germs and dust and frequently needs washing.

2. Their current washer and dryer aren't performing the way they want and they've already made the decision to buy replacements.

3. The comforter needs to be washed in a larger machine.

4. They likely have children since they have a lot of laundry.

5. They have a limited budget.

So what's going to be your response? If you want to make the sale, you need to appeal to both partners with something like, "Good morning! I see you're checking out our new washers and dryers. Did you know we have a scratch-and-dent department downstairs that offers considerable savings on many of our larger machines?" Or maybe you could explain the cost savings of buying a larger-capacity set versus a smaller, less energy-efficient one. Or you could tell the customers about current sales, promotions and even manufacturer's rebates that may make the purchase of a large-capacity machine more favorable. The key here is finding a way to make both partners happy with the sale.

Listening to Their Needs

Customers are usually pretty quick to tell you what they want and don't want. The point at which the sales process breaks down is when the sales representative fails to listen—I mean, really listen. You may have a certain monologue in your head you think will work or you may think you know what's best for the customer before you've even spoken to them, but hold on! You're not going to sell anyone anything with that attitude. A better approach is to listen to the client's concerns, needs and questions. Answer each question as thoroughly and honestly as you can. Address each concern, and show how you can satisfy each need. If you can't do any of these things, admit it and offer to get the answers or solutions elsewhere.

Use clues from the conversation, questions they ask and points they're most interested in. Make some safe assumptions from these clues. Then, take a few moments to think about what the underlying subtext is and try to address that.

For example, if you learn that the couple mentioned above does not have any children and only do a few loads per week, but are obsessed with the large-capacity washers, it could mean they've had trouble with their smaller washer and don't trust the small-capacity machines as a result. You can address this by talking about the practicality of the smaller washer for their needs and then the warranty, the way the machine is made, its dependability and so on.

Now, if they decide to buy the bigger one despite all your reasons, great. Oftentimes, customers who feel pressured by the salesperson in charge to go bigger and more expensive will fight back by resisting the sale. Those who feel the salesperson really has their best interests at heart will respond by buying what they really wanted anyway, even if it is impractical.

When you listen to a customer's needs and respond in a responsible and caring manner, the sale will go more smoothly and you may end up selling more than you expected.

Asking the Right Questions

Asking questions is a vital component to setting up a sale. Without asking the right questions, you'll never be able to figure out what your customer really wants or how to give it to them. For instance, if you notice someone looking at fragrances you might say, "Are you looking for a new fragrance for yourself or as a gift?" This will tell you right away whom the person is buying for, and then you can tailor follow-up questions to see which fragrance may be best for the recipient.

One of the biggest mistakes salespeople make is acting on an assumption when they haven't asked the right questions. For instance, just because you see a woman with several young children in tow, that doesn't mean she's only looking for family-oriented items. Maybe she wants, and needs, something completely impractical to gain some of the empowering autonomy she had before she had a family.

Listening... Again

Once you've asked the right questions, it's your job to listen to the answers and carefully consider how those answers will affect your sales approach. Be careful not to ask questions the customer can answer with a no.

Rather, ask questions that appeal to the customer's interest and can shed light on what he or she is looking for. Think of yourself as a journalist. If, when interviewing sources, journalists asked only yes and no questions, they would not get any additional information, and their stories would be boring. Your job is to investigate the customer and gain information to help you, and them.

Listening is also about being respectful of your customer's interests and needs, as well as their time. Blowing off a shopper's concerns or not taking them into consideration will only result in a lost sales opportunity.

Watching the Customer

Your prospects don't just speak with their mouths; they also speak with their bodies. A customer who crosses their arms or moves slightly away from you will not be receptive to aggressive sales tactics. In fact, it might be best to introduce yourself, let them know you're available for questions, and then move away and give them space.

A customer who leans in toward you, smiles and makes eye contact is more likely to be open, but don't abuse this openness by being pushy.

Awakening the Customer's Curiosity

This simple approach is a good way to make initial contact with a customer and make a great first impression. Be genuine and use what you've learned through this process to invigorate the sale by jumpstarting the customer's sense of curiosity and interest. As we've already discussed, these stages are absolutely necessary to get the sale, so use your approach to whet the customer's appetite and arouse their curiosity to keep them involved in the psychological process of the purchase. In short, let your appeal at this stage be entirely to the self-interest, pleasure and curiosity of the prospect. Try to warm up the individual and get their imagination working. If you do this with your initial contact, the prospect's attention is yours, and you'll have ample opportunity to make the sale.

Eight: The Presentation

The previous chapter explained how to approach a prospect and generate enough interest from them to justify asking a question or two. This should give you ample opportunity to get to a point at which you can comfortably, and persuasively, suggest a purchase. This is an important psychological stage in the buying game. It ultimately leads to the salesperson entering the presentation stage of the sales process. It's at this point the sales process changes from a passive one to an active one on the part of the buyer. Once the presentation is complete, the buyer will be in a position to discuss and consider the purchase in a more tangible way.

It makes sense this is the part in your sales strategy where you tell the client all about your product. You may be tempted to become the know-it-all who proudly announces every facet of the product or service to the point of being annoying. Resist this urge—a boring list of traits never sold anything.

A better tactic is to carefully gauge the prospect's interest and offer valuable insight into the ways in which the product or service can most benefit the buyer. As more questions or concerns emerge, you can answer them tactfully and completely.

The presentation phase of the sales process can be a bit tricky, especially when dealing with sensitive psychological keys. Push too hard and some customers will walk away; fail to give enough useful information and the client may not see a value in the purchase. Try using these basic psychological keys to find the right balance in your presentation. They've been proven time and time again to work well when it comes to keeping your sales pitch balanced.

Give Your Customers Fewer Options

People like options, but not too many. Don't fall for the mistake of giving your customers so many options they become paralyzed and unable to make a decision at all. Just because your catalogue offers thousands of products, that doesn't mean you have to show potential customers a long list of available items.

Think of yourself as part salesperson and part personal shopper. Allow one of the services you offer your customers to be separating the wheat from the chaff so they don't have to. Group similar items into subject categories and focus on these main divisions.

Think of your favorite supply catalogue. Odds are that it uses this same strategy. When you want envelopes, you go to the envelope section and review the options. When you want a new office chair, you flip to the furniture section to see what's available. Do the same thing with your customers. Instead of offering them 1,000 individual choices, highlight five or six departments or sections to give them an idea of the vast variety to choose from, without overwhelming them.

Cheaper Isn't Always Better

Sure, people love a bargain, but sometimes a bargain that seems too good to be true will turn your customers away. It's strange, but true: most people associate price with quality. If an item seems too cheap, they'll assume it's poorly made or isn't really necessary. Increase the price and watch sales soar. Why? Because the customer suddenly feels as if the product's intrinsic value is higher—what else could justify such a price? Give an item a higher price and it suddenly has more value.

People Don't Want to Miss Out

It's a psychological fact: a loss looms larger in your mind than a gain. If you can convince a buyer that purchasing your product will help keep them from losing something, such as time, money or energy, you will be more successful than if you focus on what they could gain by making the purchase.

Mystery Sells

Mystery sparks interest, and interest, as we've discovered, sparks sales. So what's the lesson here? If you can find a way to stay mysterious, then you'll drive in more business, have more opportunity to prove yourself, and, as a result, make more sales. Some sales professionals make the mistake of sharing too many personal details with their clients, assuming this "friendliness" gives them an advantage. In reality, the way you represent your personal life could work against you. Your client may find you crass, snobby, immature, too straight-laced, boring—the list goes on and on. Stay mysterious to your client and allow them to fill in their own mental picture of your personal life.

Keeping these main psychological factors in mind, you can mold your product or service demonstration to appeal to your customer while also offering the shopper some concrete information about the product or service being offered.

Let's say you're a new car sales associate. The presentation you conduct needs to include a review of the available options, statistics about the car's fuel efficiency, a maintenance review, the price, safety features and more. It should also include a test drive, during which you try to "show off" all the car's special perks. This is the time in the sales process to pull out all the stops to get the customer excited about the possibility of owning the product.

In many cases the presentation is like a game of chess. You make a move only to have the customer respond with another move. The person who makes the smartest moves wins the game. Your goal is to be the one who outsmarts the competitor and actually brings in the sale. This is most easily accomplished when you match every question and concern with an honest and thought-provoking answer. If left with nothing else to wonder, worry over or complain about, the customer has no choice but to buy. The big question is: are you up for the rigors of the game?

The back-and-forth volley can be exhausting and frustrating for some sales professionals, even those who've been in the game for a while. Those who find it invigorating are the ones who are the most successful at the game of sales. These individuals thrive on the fact that meeting a customer's resistance with a solid plan will greatly increase their odds of closing a sale.

Even during the game it's important to remember the old adage: the customer is always right. It was true 50 years ago, and it remains true now. The customer must always feel they're making the right decision, and that can only happen if you make them feel they have the upper hand in the buying process. The moment they feel like you've regained control, the sale is lost.

Instead of trying to get the upper hand, reinforce the facts and bring the buyer's attention back to the points they've already raised. Allow the customer to keep their objections, but sidetrack them by bringing out more positive points to discuss and review. In a nutshell, sidetrack and sidestep the non-essentials. This allows the customer to quickly move forward to the process of consideration. By moving the customer onto this stage, you have reinforced their belief they may want and need what you're selling. No matter how slow it goes, as long as they're still moving forward in the selling process, a sale is possible.

Too many salespeople try to make their closing talk here. That's a mistake. The customer is not yet ready to make a commitment to buy. Allow him or her to complete the psychological process, and you'll ensure a sale. Help them along by offering plenty of explanations during the presentation. This will help foster the client's imagination so they can see their ideal life, brought about as a result of the purchase.

Finally, remember to highlight enough information to whet the customer's appetite but not so much you bore them. It's better to concentrate on a few leading and striking points during your presentation and wait for the customer to ask questions before continuing with more information. Let the client lead the way, and you'll avoid taking up too much time giving details that overwhelm them or they don't care about. No matter what gets thrown at you, remain friendly, and keep a conversational style during the entire presentation. Nothing turns off a customer faster than droning on and on about boring facts and figures, even if they are important.

Five Tips for Making a Great Sales Presentation

1. Personalize your presentation: Avoid using a canned presentation that you give to every client. It won't bring excitement, enthusiasm or curiosity to the client. Present your ideas and products to individual customers in a way they can relate to.

2. Create a connection: If your prospect cannot envision how the product could serve them or make their life easier or better, they won't be inclined to buy. Find some way to connect the buyer with the product. This may even require giving them a sample or free trial to test.

3. Be succinct: Too many salespeople take way too long to get to the point when making a sales call. Don't beat around the bush. Tell the customer exactly what you're selling and why they should buy. This shows respect for their time and their intellect—and that won't go unappreciated.

4. Be creative: I can't tell you how many boring sales pitches I've sat through as the rep droned on and on without a single interesting thing to say, after which neither I nor anyone else in attendance placed an order. Think about the best and most prosperous salespeople you know. Odds are good they give a great presentation full of animation, quirks and creativity. Work to create an interesting, engaging presentation that not only gives the information the prospect needs to make a decision but that also draws them in and piques their curiosity.

5. Use a physical demonstration: Don't just stand there talking. Use a whiteboard, PowerPoint or model to deliver your points. People love to be able to see and touch things during a presentation. Find a way to let the prospect use their senses, and you're much more likely to gain their attention—and their order.

At this point, if you've done your job, your customer's imagination should be in full swing. They should be starting to see life as it would be with your product or service in place. Think this isn't important? Consider this: realtors often say the best thing they can ask for when showing a home is that the prospects start talking about where certain pieces of their furniture could be placed throughout the house. That's a sure sign a sale may be imminent because once a customer begins imagining life with the object under consideration, they begin developing an attachment to it. That attachment develops desire, which, of course, results in a sale.

Once you've completed your presentation, there's only one step left to completing the sale: the closing. Now it's time to look at that and see how it's done.

Nine: Closing the Deal

Most sales associates hate the dreaded *close*—so much so that many sales professionals actually lead the prospect right to the point bordering on a decision and action only to lose heart, leave the prospect and either bring in another person to close the deal, such as a manager, or lose the sale altogether. What a shame. By the time you reach this final step in the sales process, your job is almost complete and the sale is imminent.

It's true the close can be a bit delicate, involving some very practical psychological strategies. Still, it doesn't have to be that hard, and it's certainly not impossible. The close is simply one more step in the deal. If you've been able to keep the customer up to this point, you've laid some strong groundwork and should have no trouble closing the deal.

Factors in Closing

One of the reasons many professionals dread the close is they simply don't believe in their ability to make the sale. As the end of the process nears, they panic, begin doubting themselves, find their confidence flagging, and start to undermine all the effort they've put into the process thus far.

If the end result of all of your hard work doesn't result in a sale, ask yourself this important question: WHY? If you can figure that out, then you can make the changes necessary to finish the next deal.

When it comes to selling anyone anything, some important psychological factors come into play at the very end of the process—BEFORE the close. Here are just some of the things you must deal with in order to win the entire sales process.

- Reproduction of beliefs: If you can get the customer to want what you're selling, then you're able to successfully transfer your belief in a product to the customer. This means you've actually been able to make them see the good in the purchase.

- Influencing decisions: There is a distinct psychological moment when a customer's mindset shifts from thinking about making a purchase to deciding to make a purchase.

  o Avoiding unselling: Some salespeople simply don't know when to stop talking. They don't recognize when that shift in emotions and thought has taken place in the customer, and they continue trying to sell the product, which results in the process of unselling as the rambling strips the customer of any interest in buying.

- o Avoiding the premature close: Some salespeople are so haunted by the close they rush through it, unable or unwilling to give the customer time to process all of the information and begin to cultivate a desire for the purchase. The result: no sale. Take your time to get through each stage of the process; otherwise you risk losing the sale right at the end.

- The summation: At some point in the close, you must simply stop. This is the time when a brief summary of everything you've said takes place. Then, it's up to the customer to decide what to do: buy or walk away. This psychological moment of closing the selling talk is akin to that of a lawyer who leads the jury to a dramatic and logical climax, and then stops to let the moment have its own convincing weight.

- Avoid fiddling: Once you've made your point and the ball's in the customer's court, remain calm. Never fidget or fuss with a book or pen or appear even the least bit agitated. The customer must feel free to make a decision without distraction.

Simple Tips to Seal the Deal

Although understanding the psychological process of the sale is important, sometimes what you're really looking for are simple tips to seal the deal. Here are a few successful tips sales professionals routinely use to get the response they're looking for:

- Create a sense of urgency: Sometimes a customer is interested in finishing a deal—they just don't have the time. Create a motivating sense of urgency by offering a short-term discount, a short service agreement or some other sort of incentive. And remember, it's an incentive, not a threat.

- Use competition to your advantage: Sometimes, letting a customer know that if they don't do the deal with you, you'll find someone who will reminds them they could easily miss out on a great opportunity. This may require a good bluff, unless you do have another client in mind. Either way, letting a hesitant customer know the deal is being offered to others may be all that is needed to get them to decide in your favor.

- Be prepared not to close: The fact is some deals simply don't close. Actually, many deals don't close. That's okay. It's a perfectly normal side of business. Understanding this fact and being prepared for it will help you walk away without hurt feelings or a sense of failure.

- Always be honest: If you want to succeed in sales, the most important thing to remember is to be totally honest with your customers. Don't lie, cheat or steal to make a deal. That is a surefire way to end your career. Practice integrity and build relationships that your customers can trust. This is the only way to ensure sales success now and into the future.

Once the sale is done, remember this other important rule: stay with the client for at least 10 minutes to make sure they don't have any questions and they completely understand the purchase they've made. That doesn't mean you need to make yourself at home and overstay your welcome. Just be available to make your client feel good about the transaction they just conducted. Doing so won't just reduce your sale cancellations and returns, it will also help reduce the amount of time you spend later fielding follow-up phone calls and questions. Go through the delivery process, what the client should expect in the following days and weeks, and any other relevant information.

Ten: A Plan for Success

We've touched on the many psychological approaches to consider when making a sale, but have you considered the importance of developing a plan for your own success?

Succeeding in any business, especially sales, takes more than skill, knowledge or even a great product—it takes a plan. People act as a result of the urge of habit, authority, trial and error, or through following some plan of action. Failure to design and subsequently follow a well-designed plan will strip you of your power and keep you from attaining the success you deserve.

Plans precede reality. The fact is, where there is no vision, people perish. It's the vision people create in their mind's eye and the plans they develop that lead to the reality of success. Developing a plan of action in regard to your sales potential is the only way to achieve the kind of success you deserve.

There are several steps to developing this kind of plan:

1. Determine your objectives: What is it you want to achieve? Do you want to add to your customer base, sell more product, expand your territory?

2. Analyze the obstacles: List all the things holding you back from achieving your goals.

3. Figure out how to overcome those obstacles: What can you do to move past those obstacles or turn them into benefits?

Once you have figured out these three principles, you're ready to go after what you want.

Write out your objectives. Do not leave it to memory. Thoughts attract reality, and the best way to streamline your thoughts is to write them down where you can see them every day. It's far too easy to lose sight of the main objective simply because there are so many options vying for your attention. You start veering in another direction because seemingly good opportunities present themselves, only to discover too late that you've wandered off course. By setting your plan on paper, you'll find it easier to stay on course—especially when the road gets bumpy.

Begin by writing down your main objective, followed by the things standing in your way, and then your plans for overcoming them. For instance, maybe your main goal is to sell $1 million in product over the next 24 months. You would first list "sell $1 million" on the top of your paper and underneath list obstacles such as:

- lack of customers

- lack of advertising

- lack of confidence

Underneath those obstacles, list some things you can do right now to overcome them:

- Expand my territory to get more customers.

- Revisit old customers.

- Look into possible advertising opportunities.

You can make your plan as detailed as you want. You can list your main objectives, obstacles and solutions or you can create an in-depth five- or 10-year plan to follow to attain your dreams. As you begin traveling the road toward success, you'll gain more confidence in your abilities and increase your personal power, which will then increase your confidence and give you even more power to go after success.

Creating a plan and working toward certain goals is like building a snowball and setting it on a long course down a mountain where it will only pick up speed, momentum and power as it rolls along. You are that snowball and your journey has just begun. Life is full of possibilities. All it takes is the courage to jump off that mountaintop and begin building the power of your own personal snowball.

Every great success begins with a single step or move toward its completion. Taken one day at a time, the journey toward making your dreams a reality will materialize. It simply takes time and a little planning. Begin with a daily schedule outlining that day's action steps for increasing your sales potential. As the days and weeks pass, you will begin seeing your goals taking shape and those individual action steps leading you farther down the path toward success.

Remember that successful people

- work on Sunday to organize the week ahead;

- work during lunch;

- work early;

- work late; and

- don't work a set amount of hours each week — they work until they no longer need to get things done.

The simple fact is you are the architect of your career and your life. It's the blueprint you've been creating in this chapter that will show you what to do next in order to build the future you want.

Want to get started? Then remember these important points:

- Your aim is the general direction in which you will plan to direct your life.

- Your purpose gives you power to move forward.

- Your plan is a rough outline showing you what to do, be, see and master.

- Your schedule is a blueprint for each important move along the journey.

- Your goal is the principle objective you want to attain.

If your aim is definite, your purpose worthy, your plan wise, your schedule steadfast and your plan clean all the way through, you should be able to gain the power and strength to achieve everything you set out to accomplish!

Gaining Confidence

You need to feel good about the person you are and the contribution you're making in order for this process to work. You could be selling gold bars for $0.50 an ounce, but if you don't feel good about yourself, you won't close many sales.

One way to help gain confidence is to routinely devote time to thinking positive thoughts about yourself. When you do this, you start retraining your brain to automatically think positively rather than negatively, essentially kicking out the opportunity for negative self-talk. Keep a list of your accomplishments and the details surrounding how you contributed to them.

Review this list regularly to remind yourself you *can* do what you set out to.

Looking toward Future Success

Success doesn't come overnight, and it rarely comes without a solid plan. The first thing that must be done to achieve anything is to have a goal to aim for. Yet, far too many of us stumble through life trying our hand at this or that, never really positioning ourselves in a way that ensures real success. The fact is most people only have a dim idea of what they want and no idea how to get it.

A person destined for success knows exactly what he or she wants, figures out how to get it, and has enduring faith in him- or herself while working toward it. That may sound simple enough, but it rarely is. It takes an intelligent, enthusiastic approach that uses the small triumphs from each day to build up larger success in the weeks and months to come. Maybe you thirst for a

$10,000 sale. Understand that today's $1,000 sale is a great steppingstone toward your ultimate sales goal. However, without raising your expectations and working toward more aggressive goals, you won't ever reach those higher levels.

Eleven: A Few Final Thoughts

Becoming a successful sales associate requires a lot of things: integrity, honesty, knowledge, a sparkling personality, the ability to read a customer's mind and so on. It also requires an understanding of what makes a customer think, act and react. Unless you can come to understand and use the psychological factors associated with the sales process, you will continue to struggle to land deals and you'll find success is always a few miles out of reach.

As you work on studying this book's methods and approaches and perfecting your use of them, remember the simple rules followed by the most successful salespeople in history:

1. Be personable: Nobody wants to deal with a grumpy person or a know-it-all. Get people to like you and they will listen to what you say, which gives you a greater chance of getting them to like what you sell.

2. Be polite: Politeness goes a long way in sales. Rude, obnoxious salespeople rarely survive long, but polite salespeople thrive.

3. Get to know your customer: Until you know what your customer wants, needs and is thinking, you'll have a difficult time tweaking your sales approach to meet their expectations.

4. Understand what motivates people to buy: There are a number of different reasons one might succumb to the impulse to buy. Until you get to know those reasons, you won't be able to figure out what tactic to use with your own customers.

5. Ask questions: Asking plenty of the right questions can lead you down the path toward success by helping you better understand your customers.

6. Listen to what your customers say: Listening helps you understand what prospects want and need.

7. Offer practical solutions: People say yes to a purchase because they see value in it. They say yes because it solves a problem of time, money and/or energy.

8. Give the customer exactly what they want: Don't try to convince your customers you're offering a great deal. Find ways your product or service can fulfill a customer's need.

9. Always be honest in your sales dealings: Never lie to a customer. That is a surefire way to fail.

People only respect those they can trust. Lose that trust and you will lose the sale.

10. Know when to walk away: Not every pitch ends in success. Know when you've given it your best shot, and then walk away. If you badger the customer, you will only frustrate and anger them. Leave on good terms and you may have a shot at making a sale in the future.

Sales is a rough industry. If you're willing to learn the psychology behind it and use the tactics outlined in this book, you should be able to go out and make a sale the next time you meet with a customer or client.

Lastly, never be afraid to succeed. You can be a winning sales professional. Believe in yourself and make getting to know your product and your customer your top priorities. You won't believe how far your career will go.

About the Author

Dennis M. Postema, RFC, is a successful entrepreneur, best-selling author, coach, speaker and registered financial consultant. He is the founder of MotivationandSuccess.com, FinancingYourLife.com

StoriesofPerseverance.org, and

TheRetirementInstitute.org.

Over the past 12 years, Dennis has taught clients, agents and associates how to find motivation and ascend psychological barriers to achieve success. His dedication to improving lives has led him to work with renowned motivational and self-help industry heavyweights, such as Jack Canfield and Brian Tracy.

Dennis's personal experience with tragedy, life-changing surgeries and health issues has given him a unique perspective on what it means to achieve success and what's really standing in the way of it. He channels that perspective into educational and motivational books and programs in the topics of finance, perseverance, success and business.

His focus on helping clients, rather than simply selling products, landed him on the cover of *Agents Sales Journal* (*Senior Market Edition*) in 2011. In 2012, he was a recipient of the 10 Under 40 Award given by the Defiance Chamber of Commerce. He was also awarded the 2013 Distinguished Alumni Award from his alma mater, Northwest State Community College, for his success in the industry and community. His contribution to Jack Canfield's book, *Dare to Succeed*, earned him an Editor's Choice award.

DESIGNING YOUR LIFE

What would happen if you discovered you could do more than just live your life—you could *design* it? This book teaches you to harness the power of your subconscious and program it to help you live a happy life fitting your definition of perfection.

DESIGNING YOUR LIFE: ACTION GUIDE

These exercises help you master your subconscious, abolish negativity and raise self-esteem. This guide focuses on creative visualization and powerful affirmations, to control your life's design and master your future.

DEVELOPING PERSEVERANCE

A combination of internal roadblocks are holding you back, preventing you from persevering. This book shows you how to break through these self-imposed obstacles to begin moving along your true path, taking you further than you ever thought possible.

DEVELOPING PERSEVERANCE: ACTION GUIDE

With this guide, you'll learn about the unique roadblocks you've designed for yourself and explore the thoughts, feelings and events that impact your ability to succeed.

You Deserve to be Rich

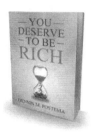

If you're busy blaming your lack of wealth on upbringing, education and environment, you're missing out on learning how easy it is to get rich. This book teaches you to throw away the excuses and focus on the 12 steps to securing a future of financial success.

You Deserve to be Rich: Action Guide

You deserve an ideal life. This workbook helps you get there by providing activities and strategies that explain the rules of greatness, help define your dreams and work to banish your fears.

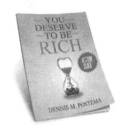

Unleash Your Mojo

You already possess everything you need to be the person you want to be, you just have to access these powerful traits. In *Unleash Your Mojo*, you'll learn to recognize all the greatness inside you and discover how to put it to use and start living your ideal life.

Unleash Your Mojo: Action Guide

Each of us has power to succeed yet many of us never tap into that power. Instead we stagnate on the sidelines while others flash forward in life. This workbook gives practical tips, advice and exercises to advance in your quest for authenticity and power.

THE POSITIVE EDGE

There's a secret behind living a happy, successful, fulfilling life: *positivity*. Learn how to overcome your tendency toward negativity, how to control your life and future, and how easy it is to improve your confidence and self-esteem.

SPARK: THE KEY TO IGNITING RADICAL CHANGE IN YOUR BUSINESS

A complete, step-by-step training program to help you become a high performer and higher earner. Learn how to rise to the top of your profession, position yourself as an expert and attract the abundance you desire.

DARE TO SUCCEED

Get motivation and information to reach the next level of success! America's #1 Success Coach, Jack Canfield, has gathered together the top business minds in one powerful book. This guide holds their strategies to conquering the competition and creating ongoing abundance.

VICTORY JOURNAL

The *Victory Journal* demonstrates the importance of writing down all your daily wins. Inside you'll find exercises to help define your ideal self and create action steps to move closer to your goals.

HARNESSING THE POWER OF GRATITUDE

Recognize the positive energy moving through your day and harness it with this undated journal. Filled with inspirational quotes to help you maintain the spirit of gratitude, it's an ideal tool for developing an enduring, powerful habit of thankfulness.

APPRECIATING ALL THAT YOU HAVE

This 365-day journal filled with inspirational quotes provides a safe space to write down the many things you're thankful for. It's the perfect way to help shift your perspective and recognize the abundance of positive forces in your life.

THE PSYCHOLOGY OF SALES: FROM AVERAGE TO RAINMAKER

Take your sales from lackluster to rainmaker without any smarm, aggressive tactics or dishonesty. This book teaches sales pros the psychology of their customers so they can present products the right way for each shopper.

THE PSYCHOLOGY OF SALES: ACTION GUIDE

In this action guide, you'll gain greater insight into your own personality and psychological makeup as well as that of your customers so you can further your sales success and transform your career.

RETIREMENT YOU CAN'T OUTLIVE

Cut through the hype and challenge conventional wisdom with a book focused on conservative and reasonable ways to save for retirement. This book uses plain language and lots of common sense that's been missing from financial planning sessions for decades.

RETIREMENT YOU CAN'T OUTLIVE: ACTION GUIDE

Transform the lessons taught in *Retirement You Can't Outlive* into action steps that change the shape of your financial future. This immersive tool contains worksheets, exercises and review sheets to help you develop a plan to rescue your financial future.

NAVIGATING THROUGH MEDICARE

Don't be confused by the rules, plans and parts of Medicare. This book simplifies the complex system and allows you to quickly and easily make the right decision for the future of your healthcare. It's a one-stop guide to everything you need to know.

AVOIDING A LEGACY NIGHTMARE

Poor planning can rip your estate from your loved ones. *Avoiding a Legacy Nightmare* is a simple guide to help you get started in creating an effective estate plan that achieves all that you intended.

PHYSICIANS: MONEY FOR LIFE

 If you want to retire on your own terms, you must understand the special considerations physicians need to make to maintain sustainable retirement plans. *Physicians: Money for Life* casts aside traditional advice that's not suited to conservative retirement planning and focuses on helping physicians design a plan that creates money for life.

PHYSICIANS: MONEY FOR LIFE: ACTION GUIDE

You have the knowledge necessary to change the financial health of your retirement, now it's time to apply it. This action guide helps you transform the lessons taught in *Physicians Money for Life* into action steps you can take to change the shape of your retirement.  With worksheets, exercises and a review, this guide will help you move forward in your retirement planning journey while devising a plan to save it.

ALZHEIMER'S LEGACY GUIDE

 Alzheimer's patients and their caregivers face a race against the clock and must learn how to cement a well-thought-out legacy plan before the disease's mental, emotional and psychological effects start to take their toll. This book provides guidance to both the recently diagnosed and those who will care for them as the disease progresses.

Financing Your Life: The Story of Four Families

This is the story of four families that took their financial lives out of the red and into the black. There's McKenna, a single mom of two boys, working hard every day as a waitress; Toby and Shannon, two professionals battling a layoff and personal spending demons; Blake and Christine, a newlywed couple in a hurry to  start living the good life, whether they can afford it or not; and Marcie and Kurt, two young parents struggling to keep up in an increasingly image-obsessed society.

Financing Your Life: The Financial Recovery Kit

 Financing Your Life is an innovative financial recovery kit devoted to teaching you how to take total control over your financial life. Within, you'll learn about the secret behind financial planning, budgeting basics, insurance, credit repair, getting out of debt, developing financial compromise with a spouse or partner, saving and investing, mortgages and more. This tool does more than just tell you about financial concepts; it helps you begin immediately integrating what you learn into your own financial life. This tool does more than just tell you about financial concepts; it helps you begin immediately integrating what you learn into your own financial life.